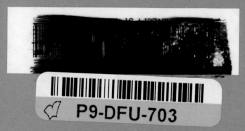
DATE		

OH, NO! Where Are My Pants?

and Other Disasters: Poems

EDITED BY Lee Bennett Hopkins   PICTURES BY Wolf Erlbruch

HarperCollinsPublishers

To Susan Pearson—
for that wonderful day

—L.B.H.

Oh, No! Where Are My Pants? and Other Disasters: Poems
Text copyright © 2005 by Lee Bennett Hopkins
Illustrations copyright © 2005 by Wolf Erlbruch
Manufactured in China by South China Printing Company Ltd.

Library of Congress Cataloging-in-Publication Data
Hopkins, Lee Bennett.
  Oh, no! Where are my pants? and other disasters : poems / selected by Lee Bennett
Hopkins ; pictures by Wolf Erlbruch.
    p. cm.
ISBN 0-688-17860-X — ISBN 0-688-17861-8 (lib. bdg.)
  1. Conduct of life—Juvenile poetry. 2. Children's poetry, American.
  [1. Emotions—Poetry. 2. American poetry—Collections.] I. Hopkins, Lee Bennett.
II. Erlbruch, Wolf, ill.
PS595.C565O38 2005
811.008'09282—dc22
                                                                    2003024272

Typography by Elynn Cohen   1 2 3 4 5 6 7 8 9 10   ❖   First Edition

CONTENTS

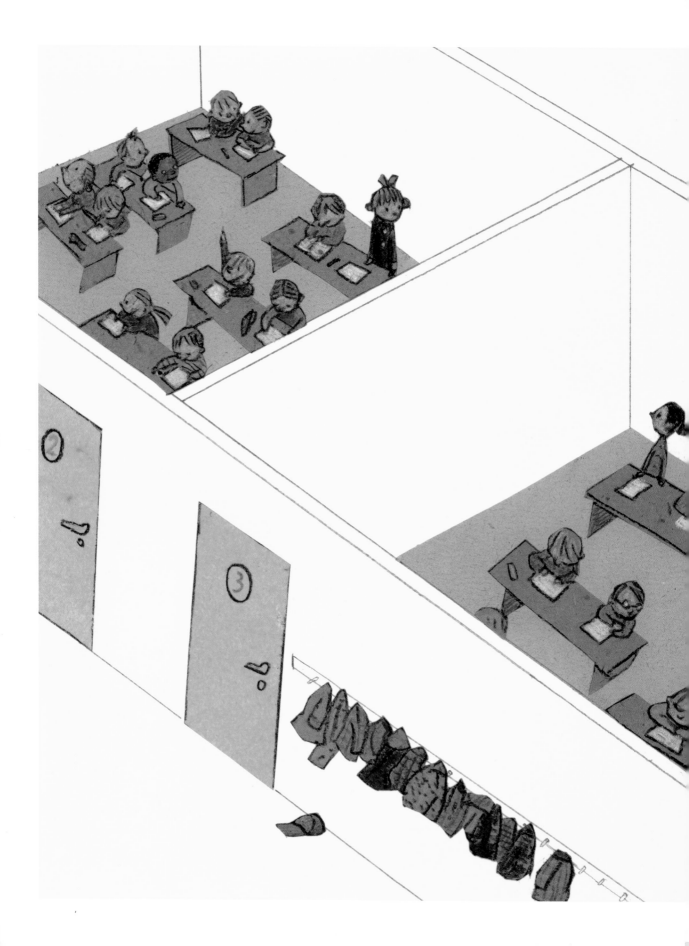

FIRST DAY

Susan Hart Lindquist

This isn't the way
it was supposed to be—
You
       in
              Room Two.
Me
      in
              Room Three.

A MILLION MILES FROM TALLAHASSEE

Alice Schertle

I was so sure
I knew the capital of Florida
I almost threw my elbow out of joint
waving my hand
in front of Mr. Miller's face.
When he called on me
I jumped up and said,
    "Tassalooma!"

I thought they'd never stop laughing.
Jerome practically
fell out of his seat.
Even Mr. Miller lost it.

Now everybody's always asking me,
    "How are things in Tassalooma?"
And Maria the comedian said,
    "Let's rent a rooma
    in Tassalooma."

And if I could go to Tassalooma—
which is nowhere
on anybody's map—
I'd never
come
back!

WINTER RABBIT

Madeleine Comora

I watched to see if he would move.
His breath was still, his eyelids closed.
There was no twitching of his nose.
"He's gone," my teacher sighed. "Today
his spirit slipped away."

I slid the latch back on his cage
that smelled of mustard greens and sage,
touched his softness to my face.
His tall straight ears, his long quick feet
trailed like falling velvet drapes.

I thought of his last night alone
huddled in a wire home.
I did not cry. I held him close,
smoothed his fur blown by the wind.
For a winter's moment, I stayed with him.

STAGE FRIGHT

Lee Bennett Hopkins

I wanted the role.
The Prince.

The Prince.

I got it.
Knew it.
I was totally convinced.

I memorized each line.
Learned them by heart.
I studied and studied
my perfect Prince-part.

But—
when I took center stage
    I stammered
    stuttered
    hemmed
    hawed
    suddenly shuddered.

My heart skipped a beat.
Face turned bright red.
Until finally
Prince-words popped back in my head.

Though I'll always know
my mind simply snapped
I still got a thrill
when I took my last bow
as my classmates
    stood up
    shouted
    and
    clapped.

AWAY AT CAMP

Ann Whitford Paul

I'm far away . . .
My bed at home's like paper no
one writes on, clean and smooth. My parents say
in letters they miss me. I don't know.
        I'm far away.

On Saturdays, who helps my father mow
the lawn? Who tells my mom which card to play
in hearts? Who laughs with her while watching TV shows?

I hate this camp! I wish there was a way
that I could be a bird and fly. I'd go
the shortest, fastest route back home. And stay!
        I'm far away.

OH, NO!

Katie McAllaster Weaver

Hello apple!
Shiny red.

CHOMP. CHOMP.

Hello worm.
Where's your head?

PLAY BALL

Joy N. Hulme

Ninth inning
score tie, full count,
one try. Bat hits with crack,
ball sails from smack, boy runs
for base. I stand in place, reach my
mitt high. Fast fly whizzes by. Where,
where, did it go? My arm way too
slow. Quick runner now races
around all four bases. His
team wins ball game.
I am to blame.

MY BRAND-NEW BATHING SUIT

Sandra Gilbert Brüg

I bought a brand-new bathing suit
    with daisies on the straps.
I wore it at the beach today
    to jump the great white caps.

A humpback wave washed over me
    and *swooshed* me all about.
It stole my brand-new bathing suit
    and now . . .
        I can't come out!

HAIRCUT

Marilyn Singer

Moments ago
    I had hair
down to there.

I could braid it
    or parade it
I had hair
    that I could wear.

Just like that
    on a dare
I lopped it
    and I chopped it
Now my head
    is nearly bare.

For a second
    I felt chic
Now I look
    just like a freak.

What will everybody say?

I wish it was still yesterday
when my hair
    my hair
        my hair
    was
long and sleek.

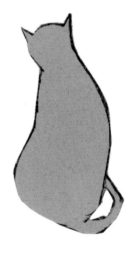

NIGHTMARE

Judith Viorst

Beautiful beautiful Beverly
Has asked me to a dance.
And I am dressed
In all my best:
My purple shirt,
My buckskin vest,
My cowboy boots,
My—oops!
Where are my pants?

AT THE STATE FAIR

Rebecca Kai Dotlich

The Ferris wheel
stops
in the air
    halfway.
My small metal seat
dangles and sways
over pink spinning teacups;
boats bobbing on lakes.
I'm trapped on top
of the world by mistake.
Kidnapped by sky,
suspended in air,
I stay very still
in this chandelier chair.
Breathless, I wait
my heart skips a beat.
Frozen, I sit
in this teetering seat.
I grip the cold bar.
My knuckles turn white.
Nothing but darkness
and moon in sight.

Bring me down, bring me down . . .

I struggle to shout
but the wheel
stands still
and nothing comes out.

MY FRIEND IS GONE

Lillian M. Fisher

A hug, a tear, and you are gone.
Your swing is missing from the lawn.
Your house is silent, dark and lone.
Your window says no one is home.
I tried hard not to cry
When you waved a last good-bye.
How will I face each empty day
Without my friend who moved away?

THE GIFT

Tom Robert Shields

My birthday's here.

I know I'll get
Those hockey skates
        this time—
        this year.

I volunteered to wash
A million dishes
Piled in our sink.

I even drew a picture
Me—
Skating at the rink.

As I ripped my present open—
Hockey dreams dissolved in air.
I couldn't believe my eyes:

A shiny brown
Pair of leather shoes
To wear!

    "Thanks, Mom,"
    I said.

    I lied.

THAT TERRIBLE DAY

Karla Kuskin

It was simply the worst
the most terrible day.
Nothing
but NOTHING
was going my way.
I would tell you the whole
of that horrible trial
but you might find it boring
or worse
you might smile.
And so, though it stuck like a burr in my mind,
and I hated my thoughts,
all in all you may find
it is better to simply
turn blank as a wall,
as I did.
Now ask me what happened.
I cannot recall.

ACKNOWLEDGMENTS

Thanks are due to the following for works herein:

Sandra Gilbert Brüg for "My Brand-New Bathing Suit." Used by permission of the author, who controls all rights.

Madeleine Comora for "Winter Rabbit." Used by permission of the author, who controls all rights.

Curtis Brown, Ltd., for "At the State Fair" by Rebecca Kai Dotlich; copyright © 2005 by Rebecca Kai Dotlich. "Stage Fright" by Lee Bennett Hopkins; copyright © 2005 by Lee Bennett Hopkins. Both reprinted by permission of Curtis Brown, Ltd.

Lillian M. Fisher for "My Friend Is Gone." Used by permission of the author, who controls all rights.

Lee Bennett Hopkins for "The Gift" by Tom Robert Shields. Used by permission of Lee Bennett Hopkins, for the author.

Joy N. Hulme for "Play Ball." Used by permission of the author, who controls all rights.

Karla Kuskin for "That Terrible Day." Used by permission of the author, who controls all rights.

Susan Hart Lindquist for "First Day." Used by permission of the author, who controls all rights.

Ann Whitford Paul for "Away at Camp." Used by permission of the author, who controls all rights.

Alice Schertle for "A Million Miles from Tallahassee." Used by permission of the author, who controls all rights.

Simon and Schuster for "Nightmare" by Judith Viorst. Reprinted with the permission of Atheneum Books for Young Readers, an imprint of Simon and Schuster Children's Publishing Division, from IF I WERE IN CHARGE OF THE WORLD AND OTHER WORRIES by Judith Viorst. Text copyright © 1981 by Judith Viorst.

Marilyn Singer for "Haircut." Used by permission of the author, who controls all rights.

Katie McAllaster Weaver for "Oh, No!" Used by permission of the author, who controls all rights.